PLANT BASED

COOKBOOK

Plant-based Recipes For Breakfast, Lunch and Dinner. Cook These Healthy Recipes To Feed Your Body And Live Well

Gianni Martini

FOREWORD

It doesn't matter what your exact goals are, but if you visit the gym, you want to see results. Weightlifters, athletes, and fitness enthusiasts usually have different objectives, but whether you want to improve strength, build muscle, increase your endurance, or trim body fat, you need to eat right. Nutrition is essential to your workout success.

If you fail to supply your body with the nutrients and calories appropriate for your fitness goals, you will never reach your full potential. That's why you want to manage your nutrition intake.

At this point of your journey, you probably need more than fuel alone – you need nutrients to guarantee enough energy to cover your basic daily activities before exercise, plus the required nutrients to guarantee muscle recovery and growth.

As harsh as it sounds, working out while following a plant-based diet means you have fewer food options than the average person. This is particularly true when it comes to the lean protein sources you need to build strength. That's why education is the best investment you can make as a vegan athlete, gym-goer, or whatever label fits you. Choosing the right foods can be challenging, but this book will make it easy.

This book will hand you the keys to proper, plant-based nutrition and its complimentary supplementation for vegans with an active lifestyle. And most importantly, we'll provide you with easy-to-store, high-protein recipes and a simple, customizable meal plan for a full month, broken down in 30 days.

The information in this guide isn't just for vegan athletes either. It's highly beneficial to anyone who wants to understand basic nutrition principles and cook tasty, healthy, easy recipes.

Table of Contents

INTRODUCTION

I didn't start developing an interest in cooking until after university, during which I subsisted on standard cafeteria food and sub sandwiches. I started buying cookbooks and experimenting with recipes—many of which were disasters. The more I created meals for myself, the more I wanted to know about making them healthier. I started on the path to more wholesome meals while I was still an omnivore, gradually steering away from meat-centric dishes.

That's where this book is different. The meal plan and recipes in this book were developed with the goal of teaching you how to make the best plant-based meals so that the food itself becomes the incentive. Because no matter your reason for switching to plants—whether it's simply to get more vegetables into your diet, lose those stubborn ten pounds, look more svelte for that special occasion, make long-term health changes as recommended by your doctor, find relief from chronic illness and symptoms, or, like me, shrink your carbon footprint by reducing your meat and dairy consumption—the reality is that if the taste of the food you eat doesn't excite you, then there is no way you will be able to maintain this way of eating, not even for three weeks.

Being a food lover doesn't have to mean feeling guilty about the foods you love. And eating to nurture your health and body doesn't mean giving up the foods you love. Being a food lover can also mean carefully choosing foods that your taste buds will love and that your body needs and craves. Plants are natural healers that, when prepared with thought and care, are fulfilling and delicious, delivering daily doses of health and happiness. By choosing plants, you are taking the first step to finding that necessary balance to eat your best, live your best, and be your best. By choosing plants, you will change your life.

The Top Ten Hints for Your Success

- Eat out, call it research

Dining out might be a luxury for some of us, but when starting a new eating plan, it can become research. Experiencing the professionals handling plant-based cuisine can inspire you to try some recipes by yourself. You can get a great sense of the great variety of flavors and possibilities that can be made without animal-based ingredients.

- Start with a plant-based breakfast

Breakfast is the easiest meal to make a plant-based. Without a doubt, you need to start the day with something energizing and nourishing. When you start with breakfast, you are more likely to move on to a plant-based lunch, then dinner, replacing all meals and snacks with plant-based ones.

- Educate yourself

Provide yourself with information from reliable sources, and consider the opinions of a reputable nutritionist so you don't have questions when starting your new lifestyle. Don't trust something just because some media, advertisements, and self-proclaimed specialists say it's a good thing. Study all peculiarities of the diet before starting it.

- Pretend boxed foods don't exist

While shopping, avoid boxed or packaged foods like they don't exist at all. Replace those foods with whole foods. Believe it or not, but such changes may even be cheaper for you. Use steel cut oats, berries, and unsweetened non-dairy milk instead of cereal, and oatmeal or quinoa in place of granola bars. Avoid "fake" meats (meat alternatives that are usually soy-based or gluten-based) and consume more edamame, lentils, tofu, and tempeh.

- Make time for meal prep

Prepare your meals for the week ahead. Spend at least one or two hours on weekends to cook a few dishes. You can prepare a large pot of grains for breakfast, roast or steam veggies for the week, boil some beans, bake some sweet potatoes and squash, and prepare a few salads so they're always on hand.

- Bring on the beans

Beans and legumes are rich in protein, potassium, fiber, B vitamins, and iron. They are nourishing and filling, and you may lose a little weight since you won't be hungry as often. Choose low-sodium or no-salt-added canned beans, as these are healthier and will save you time.

- Avoid sugar

Exclude all refined sources of sugar from your diet. Be aware of sugar in sneaky sources like sweetened non-dairy milk, hot sauce and salsa, and don't buy packaged sweets of any kind.

- Equip your kitchen

If you definitively decided to follow the plant-based food way of living, a food processor, pressure cooker, or slow cooker may really come in handy.

- Clarify your motivation

- Make a short list of the goals you want to achieve by adopting the plant-based diet. Clarify what is important to you. This list will keep up your focus and motivation in times of doubt and will inspire you for some major changes.

- Make shopping list

While shopping, follow a specific list of whole foods you need. It will keep you from buying unnecessary items, spending too much money, and getting tempted at the store. Those raw cookies and kale chips might look great, but you should avoid them and just buy some kale and fruit instead.

Mistakes and Misconceptions of Beginners

- **Myth 1**: The only way to get enough calcium to maintain strong bones is to drink milk.

- **Fact:** Many non-dairy milk alternatives exist, providing enough calcium to meet the daily rate.

- **Myth 2**: Vegetarian diets are not for pregnant women, children, or athletes.

- **Fact:** A plant-based diet includes enough nutrients for a child to be strong and healthy, an athlete to train well, keep fit, and win the competitions, and even enough for a pregnant woman to give birth to a healthy baby. The plant-based lifestyle can eliminate many unhealthy side effects of meat and dairy consumption. Plants can get you through any of life's phases.

- **Myth 3**: It's too expensive.

- **Fact:** Eating plant-based won't make a hole in your budget if you shop smart and plan your meals. Buying seasonal foods can actually help you save money. Don't be afraid to try off-brand products. Even such small trick as buying the nut pieces instead of whole ones saves some cash.

- **Myth 4:** All foods labeled as "vegetarian" are healthy.

- **Fact:** The point of a plant-based diet is to nix processed foods, so it's essential to read all labels. Many plant-based snacks, such as granola bars, often contain large doses of added sugars and oils. Pay attention to the levels of saturated fat, added sugars, and sodium when reading labels. Use raw ingredients that you know are pure.

Breakfast Meals To Start Your Day Off Right

- How many times have you eaten a doughnut for breakfast and about 10:30 a.m. your tummy starts to rumble? Those doughnuts are full of sugar, addictive sugar that just makes you want even more. Eat one and immediately your blood sugar spikes through the roof; you're revved up and ready to handle anything life can throw at you. But that's not all. Just when you've settled into your new plane of existence the mirage begins to fade. You've used up all that energy; now your sugar levels come crashing down, leaving you tired, even hungrier and grumpy because you're craving your next sugar fix.

- I'm sorry to start the chapter off with such a sad story. However, it's best to warn you up front to stay away from sugary foods in the morning and instead opt for a plant-based breakfast. It'll keep you from gnawing on the furniture mid-morning and you'll sustain your scintillating personality all the way to lunchtime.

- Now for the good news; many of the breakfast entrees in this chapter can be eaten on the go or carried with you to eat later. (Lunch, anyone?) Some you can even put together the night beforehand.

Apple Pumpkin Seed Muffins

- Apple Pumpkin Seed Muffins Will Start Your Day Off Right

This recipe calls for an apple puree that is easily made by peeling and coring three large apples and chopping them up. You'll simply toss the chunks into a blender and process the apples until they look like a bunch of lumpy baby food. You don't want to liquefy it nor smooth it out completely, because part of the delight of this muffin is biting into a small chunk of apple and getting a sweet burst of flavor.

This recipe makes six muffins. It's easiest to make in autumn when you can get raw pumpkin seeds straight out of the pumpkin. Otherwise, you'll want to use packaged pumpkin seeds that have been lightly salted or not salted at all.

Ingredients:

- 2 cups whole-wheat flour

- 1 teaspoon baking soda

- 1 teaspoon baking powder

- ⅛ teaspoon sea salt

- 1 teaspoon ground cinnamon

- ½ cup raw pumpkin seeds

- 1 cup raisins

- 1½ cups apple puree (made yourself as above)

- 1 teaspoon lemon zest

- 1 tablespoon fresh lemon juice)

- ⅓ cup maple syrup

- ½ cup almond or soy milk (adjust the amount as needed)

Directions:

- Preheat the oven to 350 degrees, Fahrenheit and prepare a muffin tin with nonstick spray or paper cupcake cups. You will use only six of the cups.

- In a bowl, whisk together the flour, baking soda, baking powder, cinnamon and salt.

- Add the pumpkin seed and raisins and stir in.

- Pour in the apple puree and combine well.

- Add the lemon zest, lemon juice and maple syrup; mix thoroughly.

- Add the milk, a tablespoon at a time, until you reach the right consistency.

- Pour the batter into six muffin cups, dividing the batter equally. Bake for 35 to 40 minutes or until a toothpick inserted in the center of one muffin comes out clean.

- Let your muffins cool for 15 minutes before removing from the pan.

- Eat warm or let the muffins cool to room temperature for future use.

Avocado Flatbread

- If you like avocados, you will love this flatbread, which you make yourself. Some of the ingredients below are only found in health food stores, but they are plant-based and gluten-free. This recipe makes four flatbreads.

Ingredients:
- ½ cup gluten-free flour

- ¼ teaspoon xanthum gum

- ½ cup tapioca starch (a.k.a., tapioca flour), divided

- ¼ teaspoon salt

- 1 tablespoon canola oil

- ½ cup water, more if needed

- 2 tablespoons avocado oil

- 1 avocado, thinly sliced

Directions:
- Whisk together in a large bowl the chickpea flour, gluten-free flour, xanthum gum, a quarter cup of the tapioca starch and salt.

- Add the canola oil and stir well.

- Add the water a little at a time while stirring, until the dough reaches the right consistency. It should be sticky and form a ball.

- Sprinkle the remaining tapioca starch on a clean flat surface and knead it into the dough. Add the starch and continue to knead until the dough is smooth and elastic. Divide into four balls.

- Roll one ball on the starched surface, flattening it and rolling it out to between six and eight inches in diameter. The shape can be round or oblong.

- Heat the avocado oil in a large skillet over medium high heat. Place the flatbread in the skillet and fry it on one side for about a minute, until the edges brown and bubble. Flip your flatbread and fry the other side. When lightly brown on the second side, remove it to a platter and repeat the process for the remaining balls of dough

- Top with sliced avocado and serve while warm.

Banana Breakfast Bars With A Blueberry Twist

- These are great for days you find yourself hitting the ground running. You can snack on one or two as you head out the door in the morning. They also make a great midmorning snack.

- The bars are sweetened with dates and apple juice. You can use either fresh or frozen blueberries with this recipe. It will make about 12 bars.

Ingredients:
- 1½ cups apple juice

- 1 cup dates, pitted and cut into half

- 3 cups old-fashion rolled oats, divided

- ¼ teaspoon nutmeg

- ¼ teaspoon cinnamon

- 2 ripe bananas, peeled

- 1 cup blueberries

- ½ cup walnuts or pecans

Directions:
- Pour the apple juice in a bowl and add the dates. Soak for 15 minutes.

19

- Preheat the oven to 375 degrees, Fahrenheit and prepare a nine by nine inch baking pan with parchment paper that extends to the top of the pan on all sides. Cut slits in the corners to allow the paper to lay flat.

- Pour two cups of rolled oats in a medium bowl and add the nutmeg and cinnamon. Whisk together until mixed, then set the bowl aside.

- Place the vanilla and bananas in the blender. Use a slotted spoon to remove the dates from the apple juice to a small bowl. Pour the apple juice and remaining rolled oats into the blender and blend until smooth and creamy.

- Add the soaked dates and pulse until chunky. You will want small chunks of date in your batter.

- Add this mixture to the blender, on top of the rolled oat and spice mixture; mix well. Fold in the blueberries and the nuts, working gently to avoid squashing the berries.

- Pour the batter into the prepared baking pan and bake for 30 to 35 minutes or until a toothpick comes out clean when inserted in the middle.

- Cool for 10 to 15 minutes before cutting into bars. Serve warm or cold; store any remaining bars in an airtight container.

Banana Peach Bread

- Quick Breads Make A Quick And Nutritious Breakfast Option

- Quick bread is easy to make and it makes for a great quick breakfast in the morning. This recipe includes both peaches and bananas, giving off a lovely aroma and a delicious flavor to wake up to in the morning. It does contain some sugar, but I use the healthier raw sugar instead of the highly processed granulated form. The batter is mixed by hand, minimizing your cleanup afterwards. This recipe makes one loaf.

Ingredients:
- 1 banana, peeled

- ½ cup canola oil

- ¾ cup applesauce

- ½ cup sugar

- 2 teaspoons vanilla extract

- 3 cups wheat flour

- 1 teaspoon baking soda

- 1 teaspoon baking powder

- 1 teaspoon salt

- 3 teaspoons cinnamon

- 2 cups diced peaches, fresh or canned and drained

Directions:

- Preheat the oven to 350 degrees, Fahrenheit and grease a regular loaf pan.

- Place the peeled banana in a large bowl and crush with a fork.

- Add the canola oil, applesauce, sugar and vanilla, stirring to mix well.

- In another bowl, whisk together the flour, baking soda, baking powder, salt and cinnamon. Gradually add and stir into the banana mixture by hand.

- Stir in the peaches and pour the batter into the prepared loaf pan.

- Bake for one and a half hours or until a toothpick inserted in the center of the loaf comes out clean.

- Cool in the pan, remove and slice.

Black Beans with Orange Breakfast Tacos

- Want something a little different, yet quite tasty, for breakfast? This will quickly become a favorite. You can easily create the filling the night before. The only thing you'll need to do in the morning is heat the filling, warm the tortillas, fill the tacos and eat them. This recipe makes about six tacos.

Ingredients:
- 1 teaspoon olive oil
- ½ cup onion, diced
- ½ cup mushrooms, chopped
- ½ cup fresh corn kernels (or frozen, thawed and drained)
- ¾ cup black beans (half of a can)
- ⅛ cup nutritional yeast (optional)
- ¼ teaspoon chili powder
- ¼ teaspoon paprika
- ¼ teaspoon sea salt
- ¼ teaspoon ground black pepper
- 2 tablespoons orange juice
- 1 package corn tortillas
- ½ cup lettuce or fresh spinach

- 1 tomato, diced

- 1 avocado, thinly sliced

Directions:
- Heat the oil in a skillet over medium high heat and sauté the onion, mushrooms, corn and black beans for four to five minutes or until they soften slightly.

- Add the yeast, if you're using it, along with the chili powder, paprika, salt, pepper and orange juice. Mash with a potato masher, but make sure to leave it slightly chunky. Stir and heat until the mixture is heated through. Cover the mixture and set it aside.

- In a skillet coated with nonstick spray, heat the corn tortillas for a minute or two on each side, just long enough to warm and slightly brown them.

- Fold the tortillas and add the filling. Top with fresh greens, tomatoes and avocado.

Chia Carrot Coconut Breakfast Pudding

- Sliced Bananas Add An Extra Treat

- I cannot adequately describe the flavor of this pudding. It is fresh, spicy and almost tropical, with a wafting of nutty flavor. All I know for sure is that it tastes scrumptious and I have a hard time stopping after one bowlful. I prepare mine the night before, so it has plenty of time to stew in its juices. All that's left to do in the morning is add a few ingredients. This recipe will give you two large bowl full or four smaller bowls. Go ahead; indulge yourself!

Ingredients:
- 1 teaspoon cinnamon

- 3 tablespoons chia seeds

- 4 tablespoons old-fashioned rolled oats

- ½ cup carrot juice

- 1 cup coconut milk

- 1 tablespoon peanut, almond, or cashew butter

- 1 banana, sliced

- Maple Syrup (optional)

Directions:
- In a bowl, combine the cinnamon, chia seeds, rolled oats, carrot juice and coconut milk. Cover and store in the refrigerator overnight.

- Remove from the refrigerator and let sit on the counter for about 15 minutes.

- Add the peanut butter and mix it in well.

- Add the sliced banana on top and drizzle with maple syrup.

Cinnamon Orange Quinoa Breakfast Pudding

- This pudding is served warm; it'll wake you up with strong flavors that pop in your mouth. The recipe does call for sugar, but I use raw sugar or a tablespoon of honey instead of granulated sugar. Agave syrup would work as well. This makes a big bowlful, which I love to share.

Ingredients:

- 1 cup quinoa

- 2 tablespoons fresh squeezed orange juice

- 2½ cups vanilla flavored almond milk

- 1 tablespoon sugar

- ¾ teaspoon cinnamon

- ¼ teaspoon nutmeg

- 1 tablespoon orange zest

Directions:

- Place the uncooked quinoa, orange juice and milk in a saucepan over medium heat.

- Stir in the sugar, cinnamon, nutmeg and orange zest.

- Let the mixture come to a rolling bowl, then let it boil for one minute.

- Turn the heat down to a simmer, cover the pot and let it alone for 20 minutes. I usually look in on the contents halfway through, just to give it a stir and check to see that it isn't burning on the bottom.

- Serve hot with more orange zest and dried cranberries or raisins sprinkled on top.

Cranberry Raisin Oatmeal

- Try Honey Instead Of Maple Syrup For A Different Flavor

Ingredients:
- 2 cups old-fashioned oats
- 1½ tablespoons raisins
- 1½ tablespoons dried cranberries
- ⅛ teaspoon sea salt
- 1½ tablespoons maple syrup
- Sunflower seeds
- Almond milk

Directions:
- In a saucepan, combine the oats, raisins, cranberries, water and salt. Stir and bring to a boil.

- Reduce the heat to medium low and stir occasionally until most of the liquid has been absorbed.

- Remove from the heat and add the maple syrup, stirring in well.

- Pour into bowls and sprinkle with some sunflower seeds and a splash of milk.

Crustless Broccoli Tomato Quiche

- This Quiche Has No Eggs, But Instead, Tofu

- This quiche is scrumptious, even though it's made using tofu and roasted vegetables. It serves four and is made in a 9-inch pie pan or a springform pan.

Ingredients:
- 1½ cups fresh broccoli, chopped

- 2 leeks, cleaned and sliced, using all the white and a little green

- 2 tablespoons vegetable broth

- 1 12.8-ounce box extra firm tofu, drained and dried

- 2 cloves garlic, chopped

- 1 lemon, juiced

- 2 teaspoons yellow mustard

- 1 tablespoon tahini sauce

- 1 tablespoon cornstarch

- ¼ cup old-fashioned oats

- 3 to 4 dashes Tabasco sauce

- ½ teaspoon turmeric

- ½ teaspoon salt

- ⅔ cup sun-dried tomatoes soaked in hot water and drained, then chopped

- ½ cup artichoke hearts, chopped

- ⅛ cup additional vegetable broth

Directions:

- Preheat the oven to 375 degrees, Fahrenheit and prepare a nine-inch pie pan by coating it with nonstick spray. Set aside.

- Cover a baking sheet with parchment paper and coat with nonstick spray. Place the chopped broccoli and sliced leeks on the sheet and drizzle with the two tablespoons of vegetable broth. Season with a little salt and pepper and toss with the hands to coat. Bake for 20 to 30 minutes until the vegetables are roasted. Remove from the oven and set aside.

- Place In a food processor the tofu, garlic, lemon juice, mustard, tahini, cornstarch, rolled oats, tobacco sauce, turmeric and salt. Process until smooth.

- In a big bowl, combine the roasted vegetables, the drained sun dried tomatoes and the artichoke hearts. Add the tofu mixture to the vegetable mixture and mix well with a rubber spatula.

- Add the broth and combine well.

- Scrape into the pie pan and flatten out the mixture. Bake for 30 to 35 minutes or until light brown. Cool for 15 minutes before slicing.

Flax meal Zucchini Cakes

- Zucchini Cakes Are Deliciously Colorful

- These pancakes contain a bunch of nutritious ingredients, things like zucchini, chickpeas and flaxseed. I serve them with a little mango chutney on top, but you can also use maple syrup or honey. This recipe serves four people.

Ingredients:
- 3 tablespoons water

- 1 tablespoon ground flaxseed

- ⅓ of a 15-ounce can of chickpeas, mostly mashed but some whole

- 2 medium zucchini, grated

- 2 tablespoons red onion, grated

- 3 tablespoons wheat flour

- ¼ cup cornmeal

- 1 teaspoon baking powder

- ⅛ teaspoon salt

Directions:

- Pour the water in a large bowl and add the flaxseed. Set aside and let soak for 10 minutes

- Mash the chickpeas and add them to the flaxseed bowl along with the red onion and grated zucchini. Stir to combine well.

- In another bowl whisk together the flour, cornmeal, baking powder and salt.

- Gradually add the flour mixture to the chickpea mixture to make a batter.

- Coat a skillet with nonstick spray and use three tablespoons each of the batter to form pancakes in the skillet. Cook each pancake for two minutes on each side and serve with chutney or syrup.

Fruit-topped Buckwheat Pancakes

- Use Any Available Fruit To Top These Pancakes

- Buckwheat flour, cornmeal and oatmeal are the base for these pancakes; they're sweetened with bananas and applesauce. Sprinkle with your choice of chopped nuts and maple syrup or top with fresh blueberries. This recipe will serve 3.

Ingredients:
- 1 cup buckwheat flour

- ½ cup old-fashioned rolled oats

- ½ cup cornmeal

- 1 teaspoon cinnamon

- 1 teaspoon baking powder

- 1 teaspoon baking soda

- ½ teaspoon salt

- 1 large banana

- 1 to 1½ cups almond milk or coconut milk

- ½ cup applesauce

- 1 teaspoon vanilla

Directions:

- Mix the buckwheat flour, oatmeal, cornmeal, cinnamon, baking powder, baking soda and salt in a large bowl and whisk to combine well. Set the bowl aside.

- Peel and mash the banana in another large bowl. Add one cup milk, applesauce and vanilla and stir to combine. If it seems too thick, add more of the milk, up to a half cup.

- Gradually add the buckwheat mixture to the banana mixture, beating with a spoon after each addition until the batter is well mixed. Let it set for five minutes.

- Heat a skillet, coat it with nonstick butter flavored spray and drop two large spoonfuls in the pan to make one pancake. Once it browns on the edges and stops bubbling, flip it to the other side and cook until brown.

- Remove to a platter and continue making pancakes with the remaining batter.

- Serve, topped with maple syrup, more applesauce, chutney, or blueberries and bananas.

German Chocolate Pancakes

- This recipe makes 12 of the most delicious pancakes ever. They taste much like a slice of German chocolate cake. The mashed banana and maple syrup are what makes the pancakes sweet. The topping emulates German chocolate frosting, made with sweet pecan butter, dates, coconut and pecans.

Ingredients:
- ¾ cup medjool dates
- ½ cup mashed banana
- 1¼ cups coconut milk
- 2 teaspoons vanilla extract
- ¼ teaspoon sea salt
- 1½ cups gluten-free flour
- ¼ cup unsweetened cocoa powder
- 2 teaspoons baking powder
- 3 tablespoons maple syrup
- 3 tablespoons pecan or almond butter
- 1 teaspoon more vanilla extract
- 1 pinch sea salt
- ⅓ cup water (more or less)
- ⅓ cup chopped pecans

- ⅓ cup shredded coconut

Directions:
- Soak the dates for 30 minutes in enough water to cover them.

- Use a food processor to lightly combine the mashed banana, coconut milk and vanilla by pulsing.

- In a bowl, mix a quarter teaspoon of sea salt with the flour, cocoa and baking powder; gradually add to the banana mixture in the processor, pulsing to combine and processing until smooth.

- Add the maple syrup while the processor is running.

- Grease a skillet with coconut oil and add the batter, a quarter cup at a time. Cook for two to three minutes on one side, then flip to cook for the same time on the other.

- Transfer to an oven-safe plate and place in a warm oven.

- Drain the dates and press with paper towels to get all the water out. Cut into chunks and put in a blender.

- Add the pecan butter, one teaspoon vanilla extract and the pinch of sea salt, blending lightly. Add enough water to make a thick but pourable topping.

- Serve the pancakes with the topping, sprinkled with chopped pecans and shredded coconut on top.

Green With Envy Breakfast Pudding

- Chia Seeds Make This Green Pudding Thick And Rich

- This breakfast pudding is green because of the spinach, which really doesn't alter the flavor but does give you a great deal of nutritional value. The date is what gives the pudding its sweetness. It tastes more like the almond or coconut milk and the fruit you put on top. The recipe makes one bowl.

Ingredients:

- 1 Medjool date with pit removed

- 1 handful fresh spinach

- 1 cup almond or coconut milk

- 3 tablespoons chia seeds

- Fruit for topping (mango, berries, kiwi, banana)

Directions:
- Place the pitted date, spinach and milk in a blender and blend until smooth.

- Pour the blended ingredients into a bowl and add the chia seeds. Stir every few minutes, letting the mixture set for a total of 15 minutes.

- Cover and refrigerate overnight.

- Remove from the refrigerator, stir and top with fruit.

Maple Glazed Pumpkin Bread

- This is another great quick bread sweetened with bananas and maple syrup. I have included a sweet glaze made with powdered sugar if you desire to use it, but the bread is tasty without anything added. The recipe makes one loaf.

Ingredients:

- ½ cup plus 2 tablespoons almond milk

- 1 teaspoon apple cider vinegar

- 1 banana, mashed

- 2 cups pumpkin puree

- 3 tablespoons almond butter

- 3 teaspoons vanilla

- ¼ cup maple syrup

- ¼ teaspoon salt

- ¾ cup wheat flour

- ½ cup old-fashioned rolled oats

- ½ teaspoon baking soda

- 1½ teaspoons baking powder

- ½ teaspoon cinnamon

- ¼ teaspoon nutmeg

- ⅛ teaspoon ground cloves

- ¼ cup chopped walnuts

Glaze **Ingredients**:
- 6 tablespoons powdered sugar

- 2 tablespoons maple syrup

- ¼ teaspoon cinnamon

Directions:
- Preheat the oven to 350 degrees, Fahrenheit and line the bottom of an oiled loaf pan with a strip of parchment paper, cut long enough to rise above the short sides of the loaf pan.

- Combine the milk with the vinegar in a small bowl and whisk well. Set the bowl aside for five minutes, until the milk starts to curdle.

- In a large bowl, whisk together the mashed banana, pumpkin puree, almond butter, vanilla and maple syrup.

- In another bowl, whisk together the salt, flour, rolled oats, baking soda, baking powder, cinnamon, nutmeg and cloves.

- Add the curdled milk to the mashed banana mixture and combine thoroughly.

- Gradually add the dry mixture to the wet ingredients, mixing well after each addition until well combined.

- Mix in the walnuts and pour the batter over the parchment paper in the loaf pan.

- Bake for 25 minutes or until a toothpick inserted into the center comes out clean. Let the bread cool for 10 minutes while making the glaze.

- Mix the glaze ingredients together and drizzle over the bread. Let this cool for at least 10 more minutes before slicing.

Mashed Potato Pancakes

- These pancakes are a little more refined than latkes, but they taste very similar. Latkes are made with shredded potatoes but these are made with mashed, so the texture is more like a regular pancake. They are super tasty served with sour cream, if you eat dairy. If you don't do dairy, you'll enjoy a topping of applesauce with a little cinnamon and stevia added. It's to die for! This recipe makes enough for four people.

Ingredients:
- 3 medium potatoes (Russet or Yukon Gold), peeled and sliced

- ½ to ¾ cup unsweetened soy, almond, or coconut milk

- Salt and pepper to taste

- 1 tablespoon parsley

- 1 tablespoon chives (optional)

- ¼ cup whole-wheat flour or rolled oats

- ¼ cup green onion, chopped

- 1 tablespoon oil or butter

Directions:
- Make mashed potatoes first or use leftovers (you'll need about two cups of mashed potatoes). You can make a fresh batch by boiling some potato pieces in enough water to cover

them, until they are soft, then draining and mashing them, along with butter and milk, if you eat dairy

- Add the parsley and chives and hand mix these.

- Add the flour or rolled oats and beat them in briefly. Don't beat the mixture too much or the pancakes will become sticky and tough. You want the mixture to look like loose mashed potatoes.

- Stir in the green onion.

- Heat a large skillet and pour in a little of the oil or butter and let melt. Drop the potato mixture by large spoonfuls and spread them with a spoon. Cook for two to three minutes on each side or until brown. Use more of the oil or butter as needed when making the rest of the pancakes, to prevent them from sticking to the pan.

- Transfer the pancakes to plates and top with sour cream, applesauce, or even maple syrup.

Eggless Breakfast Tacos

- Instead of egg, these tacos are filled with vegetables, mushrooms, potatoes, beans and quinoa for a nutritious and filling breakfast. The recipe makes four to six servings.

Ingredients:
- ½ onion, diced
- 1 handful of mushrooms, cleaned and chopped
- ½ any color bell pepper, seeded and chopped
- 1 cup cauliflower, cut into florets
- 1 large baked potato, peeled and diced
- 1 15.5-ounce can cannellini beans, drained and rinsed
- ½ cup cooked quinoa
- ½ teaspoon turmeric
- 1 teaspoon garlic powder
- ¼ teaspoon salt
- ¼ teaspoon pepper
- Corn tortillas

Directions:
- Coat a skillet with nonstick spray or add a teaspoon of canola oil or water and warm it over medium heat.

- Add the onion, mushroom, bell pepper and cauliflower. Sauté, stirring until the vegetables soften. You'll want to add a little water or canola oil if they start to stick to the pan.

- Stir in the potato, beans and quinoa; season with turmeric, garlic powder, salt and pepper.

- Spoon into tortillas, fold and serve.

Oatmeal Bars with Chocolate Chips and Pumpkin Seed

- You can Cut Into Squares Instead of Bars

- This is another bar recipe that is hard to pass up on a day when you slept in and need to get out the door quick. They also make tasty snacks. Keep the 16 bars in an airtight container and they will last about a week if you don't eat them before then. One ingredient is brown rice syrup and this, plus the maple syrup is what gives the bars their sweetness. Find brown rice syrup at your local health food store.

Ingredients:
- 1¼ cups oat flour

- 1½ cups old-fashioned rolled oats

- 3½ tablespoons pumpkin seeds

- 3 tablespoons mini chocolate chips (vegan chocolate chips or raisins instead)

- 1 teaspoon ground cinnamon

- ⅛ teaspoon ground nutmeg

- ¼ teaspoon sea salt

- ¼ cup plus 2 tablespoon unsweetened coconut milk

- 2 tablespoons maple syrup

- ⅓ cup brown rice syrup

Directions:

- Preheat the oven to 350 degrees, Fahrenheit and line an eight by eight-inch baking dish with parchment paper.

- In a large bowl, combine the flour, oats, pumpkin seeds, chocolate chips or raisins, cinnamon, nutmeg and salt.

- In another bowl whisk the milk, maple syrup and rice syrup together.

- Add the wet ingredients to the dry ingredients and pour the resulting batter into the prepared pan.

- Make cuts for the bars with a sharp knife before putting into the oven.

- Bake 20 minutes and let cool in the pan. Use a knife to cut totally through the bars.

Potato Shallot Frittata with Kick

- This frittata contains no eggs; instead it uses tofu. The flavor is excellent. You will need a deep dish pie for this one. It makes about eight wedges.

Ingredients:
- 1 tablespoon water (more if the ingredients stick)
- 2 cups potatoes (red or Yukon gold), peeled and cut into small cubes
- ¾ cup shallots, chopped
- 1¼ cups bell pepper, chopped (any color or combination of colors)
- ¾ cup unsweetened almond or soy milk
- ½ cup raw cashews
- 1 large clove garlic, minced
- 1 tablespoon fresh squeezed lemon juice
- 2 teaspoons miso
- ¼ teaspoon ground mustard
- ½ teaspoon sea salt
- ¼ teaspoon ground pepper
- ¼ teaspoon dill seed
- 2 teaspoons fresh thyme or oregano, chopped
- 1 12-ounce package extra firm tofu
- ¼ cup oat bran or gluten-free bread crumbs

- 1 pinch more sea salt

Directions:

- Preheat the oven to 375 degrees, Fahrenheit.

- In a skillet over medium heat, pour the water and put in the potatoes, shallots, salt and pepper and sauté until cooked through (about 15 to 20 minutes). Keep stirring and add more water if they start to stick.

- Add the bell peppers and cook through.

- In a blender, pour the milk, cashews, garlic, lemon juice, miso, mustard, salt and pepper. Pulse and add the thyme and the tofu. Blend until creamy.

- Remove your vegetables from the skillet to a bowl and pour the ingredients into the blender. If it seems too thick, add a tablespoon or two of milk. Pulse to mix.

- Pour the mixture into an oiled pie pan and smooth the top.

- In a small bowl combine the oat bran or bread crumbs with the salt and sprinkle over the top.

- Bake for 40 to 45 minutes and switch to broil for as long as it takes to brown the top. Let your quiche cool for 10 to 15 minutes before cutting into wedges.

Sweet Potato Breakfast Hash Browns

- Did you know that sweet potatoes are supposed to help you lose weight? They are low in calories and high in fiber, so they take up room in your stomach to make you feel full longer. Because fiber digests slower than other foods, you do not feel hungry as quickly. If I could, I would eat this every day, but unfortunately I like diversity. This recipe makes four servings.

Ingredients:
- 1 large onion, chopped

- 1 large red or green bell pepper, seeded and chopped

- 2 large sweet potatoes or yams, peeled and chopped

- ½ teaspoon paprika

- ½ teaspoon salt

- ¼ teaspoon pepper

Directions:
- Heat a non-stick skillet over medium heat and sprinkle in some oil or water. Cook the onions until they are translucent.

- Add the bell peppers and potatoes and stir to cook. Keep stirring so they don't stick to the pan. Add water if they do start to stick

- Once the potatoes are softened to your liking, add the paprika, salt and pepper.

- Make sure any liquid that may have accumulated is evaporated before you serve it up.

- The next chapter will give you all kinds of different ideas on what you can serve for lunch when you eat at home or even when you brown bag it to work or school.

Lunch Recipes
- This chapter will concentrate on lunches that are easy to make while still being delicious. Soups and salads are great on the go!

Avocado & Radish Salad

- Serves: 2
- Time: 10 Minutes
- Calories: 223
- Protein: 3 Grams
- Fat: 19 Grams
- Carbs: 10 Grams

Ingredients:
- 1 Avocado, Sliced
- 6 Radishes, Sliced
- 2 Tomatoes, Sliced
- 1 Lettuce Head, Leaves Separated
- ½ Red Onion, Peeled & Sliced
- Dressing:
- ½ Cup Olive Oil
- ¼ Cup Lime Juice, Fresh
- ¼ Cup Apple Cider Vinegar
- 3 Cloves Garlic, Chopped Fine
- Sea Salt & Black Pepper to Taste

Directions:

- Spread your lettuce leaves on a platter, and then layer with your onion, tomatoes, avocado and radishes.

- Whisk your dressing ingredients together before drizzling it over your salad.

Baked Okra & Tomato

- Serves: 6

- Time: 1 Hour 15 Minutes

- Calories: 55

- Protein: 3 Grams

- Fat: 0 Grams

- Carbs: 12 Grams

Ingredients:
- ½ cup Lime Beans, Frozen

- 4 Tomatoes, Chopped

- 8 Ounces Okra, Fresh, Washed & Stemmed, Sliced into ½ Inch Thick Slices

- 1 Onion, Sliced into Rings

- ½ Sweet Pepper, Seeded & Sliced Thin

- Pinch Crushed Red Pepper

- Sea Salt to taste

Directions:
- Start by heating the oven to 350, and then cook your lime beans. Drain them, and then get out a two-quarter casserole.

- Combine everything together, and bake covered with foil for fort-five minutes.

- Stir, and then uncover. Bake for another thirty minutes, and stir before serving.

Watercress & Blood Orange Salad

- Serves: 4

- Time: 10 Minutes

- Calories: 94

- Protein: 2 Grams

- Fat: 5 Grams

- Carbs: 13 Grams

Ingredients:
- 1 Tablespoon Hazelnuts, Toasted & Chopped

- 2 Blood Oranges (or Navel Oranges)

- 3 Cups of watercress, Stems Removed

- 1/8 Teaspoon Sea Salt, Fine

- 1 Tablespoon Lemon Juice, Fresh

- 1 Tablespoon Honey, Raw

- 1 Tablespoon Water

- 2 Tablespoons Chives, Fresh

Directions:
- Whisk your oil, honey, lemon juice, chives, salt and water together. Add in your watercress, tossing until it's coated.

- Arrange the mixture onto salad plates, and top with orange slices. Drizzle with remaining liquid, and sprinkle with hazelnuts.

Lentil Potato Salad

- Serves: 2

- Time: 35 Minutes

- Calories: 400

- Protein: 7 Grams

- Fat: 26 Grams

- Carbs: 39 Grams

Ingredients:
- ½ Cup Beluga Lentils

- 8 Fingerling Potatoes

- 1 Cup Scallions, Sliced Thin

- ¼ Cup Cherry Tomatoes, Halved

- ¼ Cup Lemon Vinaigrette

- Sea Salt & Black Pepper to Taste

Directions:

- Bring two cups of water to simmer in a pot, adding your lentils. Cook for twenty to twenty-five minutes, and then drain. Your lentils should be tender.

- Bring another pot of salted water to a boil, and add in your potatoes. Reduce to a simmer, cooking for fifteen minutes, and then drain. Halve your potatoes once they're cool enough to touch.

- Put your lentils on a serving plate, and then top with scallions, potatoes and tomatoes. Drizzle with your vinaigrette, and season with salt and pepper.

Edamame Salad

- Serves: 1

- Time: 15 Minutes

- Calories: 299

- Protein: 20 Grams

- Fat: 9 Grams

- Carbs: 38 Grams

Ingredients:
- ¼ Cup Red Onion, Chopped

- 1 Cup Corn Kernels, Fresh

- 1 Cup Edamame Beans, Shelled & Thawed

- 1 Red Bell Pepper, Chopped

- 2-3 Tablespoons Lime Juice, Fresh

- 5-6 Basil Leaves, Fresh & Sliced

- 5-6 Mint Leaves, Fresh & Sliced

- Sea Salt & Black Pepper to Taste

Directions:
- Place everything into a Mason jar, and then seal the jar tightly. Shake well before serving.

Cauliflower & Apple Salad

- Serves: 4

- Time: 25 Minutes

- Calories: 198

- Protein: 7 Grams

- Fat: 8 Grams

- Carbs: 32 Grams

Ingredients:
- 3 Cups Cauliflower, Chopped into Florets

- 2 Cups Baby Kale

- 1 Sweet Apple, Cored & Chopped

- ¼ Cup Basil, Fresh & Chopped

- ¼ Cup Mint, Fresh & Chopped

- ¼ Cup Parsley, Fresh & Chopped

- 1/3 Cup Scallions, Sliced Thin

- 2 Tablespoons Yellow Raisins

- 1 Tablespoon Sun Dried Tomatoes, Chopped

- ½ Cup Miso Dressing, Optional

- ¼ Cup Roasted Pumpkin Seeds, Optional

Directions:
- Combine everything together, tossing before serving.

Olive & Fennel Salad

- Serves: 3

- Time: 5 Minutes

- Calories: 331

- Protein: 3 Grams

- Fat: 29 Grams

- Carbs: 15 Grams

Ingredients:
- 6 Tablespoons Olive Oil

- 3 Fennel Bulbs, Trimmed, Cored & Quartered

- 2 Tablespoons Parsley, Fresh & Chopped

- 1 Lemon, Juiced & Zested

- 12 Black Olives

- Sea Salt & Black Pepper to Taste

Directions:
- Grease your baking dish, and then place your fennel in it. Make sure the cut side is up.

- Mix your lemon zest, lemon juice, salt, pepper and oil, pouring it over your fennel.

- Sprinkle your olives over it, and bake at 400.

- Serve with parsley.

Red Pepper & Broccoli Salad

- Serves: 2

- Time: 15 Minutes

- Calories: 185

- Protein: 4 Grams

- Fat: 14 Grams

- Carbs: 8 Grams

Ingredients:
- Ounces Lettuce Salad Mix

- 1 Head Broccoli, Chopped into Florets

- 1 Red Pepper, Seeded & Chopped

- Dressing:

- 3 Tablespoons White Wine Vinegar

- 1 Teaspoon Dijon Mustard

- 1 Clove Garlic, Peeled & Chopped Fine

- ½ Teaspoon Black Pepper

- ½ Teaspoon Sea Salt, Fine

- 2 Tablespoons Olive Oil

- 1 Tablespoon Parsley, Chopped

Directions:
- Blanch your broccoli in boiling water, and then drain it. Drain it on a paper towel.

- Whisk together all dressing ingredients.

- Toss ingredients together before serving.

Zucchini & Lemon Salad

- Serves: 2

- Time: 3 Hours 10 Minutes

- Calories: 159

- Protein: 3 Grams

- Fat: 14 Grams

- Net Carbs: 7 Grams

Ingredients:

- 1 Green Zucchini, Sliced into Rounds

- 1 Yellow Squash, Zucchini, Sliced into Rounds

- 1 Clove Garlic, Peeled & Chopped

- 2 Tablespoons Olive Oil

- 2 Tablespoons Basil, Fresh

- 1 Lemon, Juiced & Zested

- ¼ Cup Coconut Milk

- Sea Salt & Black Pepper to Taste

Directions:
- Toss all of your ingredients in a bowl, refrigerating for three hours before serving.

Mediterranean Wrap

- Serves: 1

- Time: 10 Minutes

- Calories: 428

- Protein: 13 Grams

- Fat: 23 Grams

- Carbs: 47 Grams

Ingredients:
- ¼ Cup Crispy Chickpeas

- ¼ Cup Cherry Tomatoes, Halved

- Handful Baby Spinach

- 2 Romaine Lettuce Leaves for Wrapping

- 2 Tablespoons Lemon Juice, Fresh

- ¼ Cup Hummus

- 2 Tablespoons Kalamata Olives, Quartered

Directions:
- Mix everything but your lettuce leaves and hummus together.

- Put your hummus on your lettuce leaves, topping with your chickpea mixture, and then serve immediately.

Quinoa with Nectarine Slaw

- Serves: 2

- Time: 20 Minutes

- Calories: 396

- Protein: 11 Grams

- Fat: 18 Grams

- Carbs: 52 Grams

Ingredients:
- ½ Cup Kale, Chopped

- 1/3 Cup Pumpkin Seeds, Roasted

- 3 Tablespoons Lemon Vinaigrette

- 1 Teaspoon Nutritional Yeast (Optional)

- 1/3 Cup Scallions, Sliced Thin

- 1 Cup Quinoa, Cooked & Room Temperature

- 2 Nectarines, Chopped into ½ Inch Wedges

- ½ Cup White Cabbage, Shredded

Directions:
- Combine everything together in a bowl before serving.

Summer Chickpea Salad

- Serves: 4

- Time: 15 Minutes

- Calories: 145

- Protein: 4 Grams

- Fat: 7.5 Grams

- Carbs: 16 Grams

Ingredients:
- 1 ½ Cups Cherry Tomatoes, Halved

- 1 Cup English Cucumber, Slices

- 1 Cup Chickpeas, Canned, Unsalted, Drained & Rinsed

- 1/3 Cup Flat Leaf Parsley, Roughly Chopped

- ¼ Cup Red Onion, Slivered

- 2 Tablespoon Olive Oil

- 1 ½ Tablespoon Lemon Juice, Fresh

- 1 ½ Tablespoon Lemon Juice, Fresh

- Sea Salt & Black Pepper to Taste

Directions:
- Mix everything together, and toss to combine before serving.

Corn & Black Bean Salad

- Salad: 6

- Time: 10 Minutes

- Calories: 159

- Protein: 6.4 Grams

- Fat: 5.6 Grams

- Carbs: 23.7 Grams

Ingredients:

- ¼ Cup Cilantro, Fresh & Chopped

- 1 Can Corn, Drained (10 Ounces)

- 1/8 Cup Red Onion, Chopped

- 1 Can Black Beans, Drained (15 Ounces)

- 1 Tomato, Chopped

- 3 Tablespoons Lemon Juice, Fresh

- 2 Tablespoons Olive Oil

- Sea Salt & Black Pepper to Taste

Directions:
- Mix everything together, and then refrigerate until cool. Serve cold.

Parsley Salad

- Serves: 8

- Time: 30 Minutes

- Calories: 165.2

- Protein: 3.8 Grams

- Fat: 9.1 Grams

- Carbs: 20.1 Grams

Ingredients:
- 3 Lemons, Juiced

- 150 Grams Flat Lea Parsley, Chopped Fine

- 1 Cup Boiled Water

- 5 Tablespoons Olive Oil

- Sea Salt & Black Pepper to Taste

- 6 Green Onions, Chopped Fine

- 1 Cup Bulgur

- 4 Tomatoes, Chopped Fine

Directions:

- Add your Bulgur to your water, and mix well. Put a towel on top of it to steam it. Keep it to the side, and then chop your spring onions, tomatoes and parsley. Put them in your salad bowl.

- Pour your juice into the mixture, and then add in your olive oil, salt and pepper.

- Put this mixture over your bulgur to serve.

Red Lentil Soup

- Serves: 4

- Time: 50 Minutes

- Calories: 188

- Protein: 12.5 Grams

- Fat: 1.2 Grams

- Carbs: 33.6 Grams

Ingredients:
- 1 Teaspoon Paprika

- 4 Cups Vegetable Stock

- ¼ Cup Onion, Chopped Fine

- 1 Cup Lentil, Red, Washed & Cleaned

- ½ Cup Potato, Peeled & Diced

- Sea Salt & Black Pepper to Taste

Directions:
- Rinse your lentils under cold water, and then get out a medium pot.

- Place your red lentils, potatoes, stock, onion and paprika in the pot.

- Bring it to a boil, and then decrease the heat to allow it to simmer.

- Put the lid on loosely, and cook until your lentils are tender. This will take roughly thirty minutes.

- Add your salt and pepper, put a cup of the soup in the food processor, and then place the blended soup back into the pot.

- Serve warm.

Mac & "Cheese"

- Serves: 6

- Time: 40 Minutes

- Calories: 848

- Protein: 70 Grams

- Fat: 8.4 Grams

- Carbs: 140.1 Grams

Ingredients:
- Milk Substitute

- 16 Ounces Elbow Macaroni, Whole Wheat

- 16 Ounces Vegan Mayonnaise

- 3 Cups Nutritional Yeast

- Whole Wheat Bread Crumbs

- Sea Salt & Black Pepper to Taste

Directions:

- Start by heating your oven to 350, and then make your noodles as the package instructs. Drain them, and then add in your ingredients, and mix well.

- Add in your milk substitute, stirring until creamy.

- Pour your ingredients into a baking dish and then sprinkle your bread crumbs on top.

- Bake until it's golden brown, which will take about a half hour.

-

Thai Squash Soup

- Serves: 2

- Time: 30 Minutes

- Calories: 717.3

- Protein: 10.3 Grams

- Fat: 48.3 Grams

- Carbs: 77.4 Grams

Ingredients:
- 1 Teaspoon Curry Powder

- 1 Tablespoon Olive Oil

- 1 Red Onion, Chopped

- 1 Pint Vegetable Stock

- 1 Butter Squash, Chunked

- 1 Can Coconut Milk (Roughly 13.5 Ounces)

Directions:

- Get out a pan and heat your olive oil. Once it's heated, add in your onion and cook to soften. This should take two to three minutes. Add your butternut squash, stock to taste, and curry powder.

- Bring it to a boil, and then reduce to simmer. The squash should become tender.

- Stir in your coconut milk, and then blend until smooth.

- Return it to the pan to warm, and season with salt and pepper before serving.

-

Butter Bean Hummus

- Serves: 4

- Time: 5 Minutes

- Calories: 150

- Protein: 8 Grams

- Fat: 4 Grams

- Carbs: 23 Grams

Ingredients:
- 1 Can Butter Beans, Drained & Rinsed

- 4 Sprigs Parsley, Minced

- 1 Tablespoon Olive Oil

- ½ Lemon, Juiced

- 2 Cloves Garlic, Minced

- Sea Salt to Taste

Directions:
- Blend all of your ingredients together, and then serve as a dip with fresh vegetables.

Spinach & Orange Salad

- Serves: 6

- Time: 15 Minutes

- Calories: 99

- Protein: 2.5 Grams

- Fat: 5 Grams

- Carbs: 13.1 Grams

Ingredients:
- ¼ -1/3 Cup Vegan Dressing

- 3 Oranges, Medium, Peeled, Seeded & Sectioned

- ¾ lb. Spinach, Fresh & Torn

- 1 Red Onion, Medium, Sliced & Separated into Rings

Directions:
- Toss everything together, and serve with dressing.

Lentil & Sweet Potato Soup

- Serves: 6

- Time: 40 Minutes

- Calories: 323

- Protein: 16 Grams

- Fat: 3.4 Grams

- Carbs: 58.5 Grams

Ingredients:
- 1 Cup Red Lentil

- 750 Grams Sweet Potatoes

- ¼ Teaspoon Cayenne

- 3 Onions

- 1 lemon

- 5 Cloves Garlic

- ½ Teaspoon Turmeric

- ½ Cup Coriander, Chopped

- 5 Cups of water

- 2 Teaspoon Cumin

- Sea Salt & Black Pepper to Taste

Directions:

- Start by peeling and chopping your onion and sweet potatoes, and it can be a little thick.

- Combine your garlic, water, lentils, cumin, turmeric and cumin together in a pot.

- Bring it to a boil, and allow it to simmer for a half hour.

- Puree your soup before adding in your lemon juice and coriander. Season with salt and pepper to taste.

Fruity Kale Salad

- Serves: 4

- Time: 30 Minutes

- Calories: 220

- Protein: 4 Grams

- Fat: 17 Grams

- Carbs: 16 Grams

Ingredients:
- Salad:

- 10 Ounces Baby Kale

- ½ Cup Pomegranate Arils

- 1 Tablespoon Olive Oil

- 1 Apple, Sliced

- Dressing:

- 3 Tablespoons Apple Cider Vinegar

- 3 Tablespoons Olive Oil

- 1 Tablespoon Tahini Sauce (Optional)

- Sea Salt & Black Pepper to Taste

Directions:

- Wash and dry the kale. If kale is too expensive, you can also use lettuce, arugula or spinach. Take the stems out, and chop it.

- Combine all of your salad ingredients together.

- Combine all of your dressing ingredients together before drizzling it over the salad to serve.

Black Eyed Peas Stew

- Serves: 5

- Time: 30 Minutes

- Calories: 338

- Protein: 21 Grams

- Fat: 4 Grams

- Carbs: 58 Grams

Ingredients:
- 1 Can Tomatoes, Crushed

- ¼ Teaspoon Cayenne

- 1 Clove Garlic

- 2 Tablespoons Olive Oil

- 1 Onion

- 2 Cans Black Eyed Peas, Drained

- 8 Ounces Okra, Frozen & Thawed

- Sea Salt to Taste

Directions:
- Start by brown your onion using olive oil, and then add in your garlic and cayenne. Cook for another minute.

- Mix in all of your remaining ingredients, simmering until your okra becomes soft.

White Bean & Spinach Soup

- Serves: 4

- Time: 25 Minutes

- Calories: 218

- Protein: 12 Grams

- Fat: 3.3 Grams

- Carbs: 37.9 Grams

Ingredients:

- 3 Cups Baby Spinach, Cleaned & Trimmed

- 1 Can White Beans (Roughly 14.5 Ounces)

- 3-4 Cups Vegetable Stock, Homemade

- 1 Shallot, Diced Fine

- 1 Clove Garlic, Minced Fine

- 14.5 Ounces Tomatoes, Diced

- 1 Teaspoon Rosemary

- ½ Cup Shell Pasta, Whole Wheat

- 2 Teaspoons Olive Oil

- Red Pepper Flakes to Taste

- Black Pepper to Taste

Directions:

- Start by heating your olive oil in a saucepan before sautéing your garlic and shallots

- Add in your rosemary, beans, broth and tomatoes. Season with your red pepper flakes and black pepper.

- Put your pasta in, cooking for ten minutes, and then add in your spinach. Cook until it's wilted.

DINNER

Summer Harvest Pizza

- Prep time: 20 minutes

- Cooking time: 15 minutes

- Servings: 2

- Nutritional Information:

- Carbohydrates – 23 g

- Fat – 15 g

- Protein – 11 g

- Calories – 230

Ingredients:
- 1 Lavash flatbread, whole grain

- 4 Tbsp Feta spread, store-bought

- ½ cup cheddar cheese, shredded

- ½ cup corn kernels, cooked

- ½ cup beans, cooked

- ½ cup fire-roasted red peppers, chopped

Instructions:
- Preheat oven to 350°F.

- Cut Lavash into two halves. Bake crusts on a pan in the oven for 5 minutes.

- Spread feta spread on both crusts. Top with remaining ingredients.

- Bake for another 10 minutes.

- Note. For ovo-lacto vegetarian, lacto vegetarian, pescatarian diets.

Whole Wheat Pizza with Summer Produce

- Prep time: 15 minutes
- Cooking time: 15 minutes
- Servings: 2
- Nutritional Information:
- Carbohydrates – 66 g
- Fat – 18 g
- Protein – 17 g

- Calories – 470

Ingredients:

- 1 pound whole wheat pizza dough
- 4 ounces goat cheese
- ⅔ cup blueberries
- 2 ears corn, husked
- 2 yellow squash, sliced
- 2 Tbsp olive oil

Instructions:

- Preheat the oven to 450°F.
- Roll the dough out to make a pizza crust.
- Crumble the cheese on the crust. Spread remaining ingredients, then drizzle with olive oil.
- Bake for about 15 minutes. Serve.
- Note. For ovo-lacto vegetarian, lacto vegetarian, pescatarian diets.

Spicy Chickpeas

- Prep time: 15 minutes
- Cooking time: 20 minutes
- Servings: 8
- Nutritional Information:
- Carbohydrates – 25 g
- Fat – 3 g
- Protein – 5 g

- Calories – 146

Ingredients:
- 1 Tbsp extra-virgin olive oil
- 1 yellow onion, diced
- 1 tsp curry
- ¼ tsp allspice
- 1 can diced tomatoes
- 2 cans chickpeas, rinsed, drained
- Salt, cayenne pepper, to taste

Instructions:
- Simmer onions in 1 Tbsp oil for 4 minutes.
- Add allspice and pepper, cook for 2 minutes.
- Stir in tomatoes, and cook for another 2 minutes.
- Add chickpeas, and simmer for 10 minutes.
- Season with salt, and serve.

Farro with Pistachios & Herbs

- Prep time: 20 minutes

- Cooking time: 45 minutes

- Servings: 10

- Nutritional Information:

- Carbohydrates – 30 g

- Fat – 9 g

- Protein – 8 g

- Calories – 220

Ingredients:
- 2 cups farro

- 4 cups of water

- 1 tsp kosher salt, divided

- 2 ½ Tbsp extra-virgin olive oil

- 1 onion, chopped

- 2 cloves garlic, minced

- ½ tsp ground pepper, divided

- ½ cup parsley, chopped

- 4 oz salted shelled pistachios, toasted, chopped

Instructions:
- Combine farro, water, and ¾ tsp salt, simmer for 40 minutes.

- Cook onion and garlic in 2 Tbsp oil for 5 minutes.

- Combine ½ tsp oil, ¼ tsp pepper, parsley, pistachios, and toss well.

- Combine all. Season with salt and pepper.

Millet and Teff with Squash & Onions

- Prep time: 10 minutes

- Cooking time: 20 minutes

- Servings: 6

- Nutritional Information:

- Carbohydrates – 40 g

- Fat – 2 g

- Protein – 6 g

- Calories – 200

Ingredients:

- 1 cup millet

- ½ cup teff grain

- 4½ cups of water

- 1 onion, sliced

- 1 butternut squash, chopped

- Sea salt, to taste

Instructions:
- Rinse millet, and put in a large pot.

- Add remaining ingredients. Mix well.

- Simmer 20 minutes until all the water is absorbed.

- Serve hot.

Brown Rice Tabbouleh

- Prep time: 20 minutes

- Cooking time: 0 minutes

- Servings: 6

- Nutritional Information:

- Carbohydrates – 25 g

- Fat – 10 g

- Protein – 3 g

- Calories – 201

Ingredients:
- 3 cups brown rice, cooked

- ¾ cup cucumber, chopped

- ¾ cup tomato, chopped

- ¼ cup mint leaves, chopped

- ¼ cup green onions, sliced

- ¼ cup olive oil

- ¼ cup lemon juice

- Salt, pepper, to taste

Instructions:
- Combine all ingredients in a large bowl.

- Toss well and chill for 20 min.

Healthy Hoppin' John

- Prep time: 15 minutes

- Cooking time: 1 hour

- Servings: 4

- Nutritional Information:

- Carbohydrates – 47 g

- Fat – 5 g

- Protein – 6 g

- Calories – 248

Ingredients:
- 1 Tbsp extra-virgin olive oil

- 1 onion, diced

- 2 garlic cloves, minced

- 1 cup of dried black-eyed peas

- 1 cup brown rice, uncooked

- 4 cups of water

- Salt, pepper, to taste

Instructions:
- Cook the onions and garlic in oil for 3 minutes.

- Combine the peas, salt, brown rice, and 4 cups of water and bring to a boil.

- Add pepper. Simmer for 45 minutes.

- Serve hot.

Mango & Papaya After-Chop

- Prep time: 25 minutes
- Cooking time: 0 minutes
- Servings: 1
- Nutritional Information:
- Carbohydrates – 25 g
- Fat – 1 g
- Protein – 1 g
- Calories – 100

Ingredients:
- ¼ of papaya, chopped
- 1 mango, chopped

- 1 Tbsp coconut milk

- ½ tsp maple syrup

- 1 Tbsp peanuts, chopped

Instructions:
- Cut open the papaya. Scoop out the seeds, chop.

- Peel the mango. Slice the fruit from the pit, chop.

- Put the fruit in a bowl. Add remaining ingredients. Stir to coat.

Sautéed Bosc Pears with Walnuts

- Prep time: 15 minutes

- Cooking time: 16 minutes

- Servings: 6

- Nutritional Information:

- Carbohydrates – 31 g

- Fat – 10 g

- Protein – 2 g

- Calories – 220

Ingredients:
- 2 Tbsp salted butter

- ¼ tsp cinnamon

- ¼ tsp nutmeg, ground

- 6 Bosc pears, peeled, quartered

- 1 Tbsp lemon juice

- ½ cup walnuts, chopped, toasted

Instructions:
- Melt butter in a skillet, add spices and cook for 30 seconds.

- Add pears and cook for 15 minutes. Stir in lemon juice.

- Serve topped with walnuts.

Brown Rice Pudding

- Prep time: 5 minutes

- Cooking time: 1 hour 30 minutes

- Servings: 6

- Nutritional Information:

- Carbohydrates – 52 g

- Fat – 10 g

- Protein – 5 g

- Calories – 330

Ingredients:
- 2 cups brown rice, cooked

- 3 cups light coconut milk

- 3 eggs

- 1 cup brown sugar

- 1 tsp vanilla

- ½ tsp salt

- ½ tsp cinnamon

- ¼ tsp nutmeg

Instructions:
- Blend all ingredients well. Put mixture in a 2-quart casserole dish.

- Bake at 300°F for 90 minutes.

- Serve.

Raw Energy Squares

- Prep time: 30 minutes

- Cooking time: 0 minutes

- Servings: 6

- Nutritional Information:

- Carbohydrates – 52 g

- Fat – 10 g

- Protein – 5 g

- Calories – 330

Ingredients:
- 2 cups moist Medjool dates, pitted and chopped

- 2 cups cashews

- ½ cup almonds

- ¾ cup cocoa powder

- Sea salt, to taste

- 2 Tbsp vanilla extract

- 3 Tbsp cold water

Instructions:
- Blend first five ingredients in a food processor.

- Add the vanilla and water, give a quick pulse.

- Put the dough into a pan, making an even layer.

- Cut into squares and serve.

Spiced Pecans

- Prep time: 15 minutes

- Cooking time: 15 minutes

- Servings: 12

- Nutritional Information:

- Carbohydrates – 6 g

- Fat – 24 g

- Protein – 2 g

- Calories – 232

Ingredients:
- 2 Tbsp brown sugar

- ½ tsp sweet paprika

- ½ tsp chili powder

- ½ cup butter, melted

- 4 cups pecans

Instructions:
- Preheat oven to 350°F.

- Blend first five ingredients.

- Pour in the butter and mix. Add the nuts and toss to coat.

- Spread the seasoned nuts on a baking sheet. Roast for 15 minutes.

Date Porcupines

- Prep time: 20 minutes

- Cooking time: 15 minutes

- Servings: 18

- Nutritional Information:

- Carbohydrates – 8 g

- Fat – 1 g

- Protein – 1 g

- Calories – 114

Ingredients:
- 2 eggs

- 1 Tbsp extra-virgin olive oil

- 1 tsp vanilla

- 1 cup Medjool dates, pitted, chopped

- 1 cup walnuts, chopped

- ¾ cup flour

- 1 cup coconut, shredded

- ½ tsp salt

Instructions:
- Preheat oven to 350°F.

- Beat the eggs, adding the oil and vanilla. Fold in the dates and walnuts. Add flour and salt to the mixture, mix well.

- Form the mixture into small balls and roll in coconut. Bake for 15 minutes.

- Serve cold.

Banana Muffins

- Prep time: 15 minutes

- Cooking time: 20 minutes

- Servings: 18

- Nutritional Information:

- Carbohydrates – 8 g

- Fat – 1 g

- Protein – 1 g

- Calories – 108

Ingredients:

- 3 bananas

- 2 eggs

- 2 cups whole wheat pastry flour

- ⅓ cup sugar

- 1 tsp salt

- 1 tsp baking soda

- ½ cup walnuts, chopped

Instructions:
- Preheat oven to 350°F.

- Grease and flour 10 cups of a muffin tin.

- Mix bananas and eggs together. Add sifted dry ingredients.

- Add nuts. Mix well.

- Spoon into muffin tins. Bake for 20 minutes.

Conclusion

You are now well on your way to eating great while fueling your body with the healthy nutrients needed to live a productive and energy charged life! The recipes in this book are all plant-based and delicious. Here, we've covered your whole day, from the time you wake up to midnight snacks. You now have at your disposal everything you need to get started on the path towards a healthier way of living. By reducing or eliminating meat from your diet, you can not only feel better, but you can be confident that you are fueling yourself, family and friends with delicious meals that can bring vibrant health.

Now it's time to begin frequenting the produce section of your local grocery store – if you haven't already. It will make you healthier in the long run and will enable you to live a more energy filled life. Revisit the first couple chapters of this book to refresh your memory on which foods are the most helpful to you in your pursuit of great plant-based meals. Swap out one unhealthy food item each week that you know is not helping you and put in its place one of the plant-based ingredients that you like. Then have some fun creating the many different recipes in this book. Find out what recipes you like the most so you can make them often and most of all; have some fun exploring all your recipe options.

61339104R00080

Made in the USA
Middletown, DE
18 August 2019